From Small Talk to...

Smart Talk

12 Keys to Becoming a Successful Communicator

Dawn Lehman, M.S., M.B.A.

Hughes Henshaw Publications
Denver, Colorado

ISBN 1-892693-16-X

Library of Congress Cataloging-in-Publication Data

Printed in the United States of America
C&M Press
Denver, Colorado

For my brother, Marcus Lehman, who rises to the challenge of communicating every day.

Contents

From Small Talk to...

Smart Talk

12 Keys to Becoming a Successful Communicator

Introduction

"I hadn't learned yet what I know now -
that the ability to communicate is everything."

Lee Iacocca, former Chrysler chairman

Have you ever felt embarrassed because you couldn't keep a conversation going with someone you needed to impress? Or left out because you weren't able to get your ideas across at a meeting? Or terrified, because you were supposed to mingle with a roomful of strangers who could be important to your business success?

These are all situations where you need *smart talk*. Your ability to say the right thing at the right time can be the deciding factor for the level of success you achieve in your business and personal life.

You are constantly being judged by what you say and how you say it. Whether you want a raise from your boss,

3

cooperation from employees, or rapport with customers, your success will depend on how effective you are as a communicator. Even more important, your satisfaction and enjoyment from your job will depend on it. If you can't create a connection with the colleagues and clients you work with, your Monday through Friday existence will become so dreary that one day you will "take that job and shove it," as the song goes, or more likely, your employer or customer will do the shoving for you.

That is why you need to understand and practice the twelve *smart talk* keys that are in this book. Instead of feeling frustrated by not knowing what to say, or wishing you had said something else, you will learn easy techniques to apply when you are:

- Talking One-On-One
- Talking In Groups
- Talking at Large Gatherings

Most of us were never taught these *smart talk* skills in our formal schooling. Instead, we had to pick them up as we went along, and many of us did not pick up the ones we needed.

We often feel that we are missing something, but the best we can do is look at someone else and say, "I wish I could talk like that." We don't know what that person is doing that makes him or her effective.

This book will take the mystery out of the conversations you see working so well for others. We will begin with *one-on-one communication* between you and another person. Your confidence will grow as you discover how to find your own communication style, how to build rapport with colleagues and customers, how to listen to them, and how to handle conflict with finesse.

Then we will move on to *talking in groups*. Meetings will become more fun as you learn how to speak up and get your point across, how to support others when they have the floor, how to keep one person from dominating the floor, how to choose an effective role for yourself, and how to handle office politics to your advantage.

Finally, we will focus on *talking at large gatherings*. The mystery of successful mingling will disappear as you learn how to identify your purpose for attending events, how to work a room like a pro, and how to make the contacts you need.

All these *smart talk* skills can be applied to both your professional and personal life, so you can use them whenever you communicate with others.

Eleanor Roosevelt said, "No one can make you feel inferior without your consent." There is no need to doubt yourself when you communicate. Saying the right thing at the right time is something you can learn to do. Read and practice the twelve *smart talk* keys that follow, and you will be on your way to becoming the successful communicator you were meant to be.

Notes to Yourself:

In what situations have you felt inadequate as a communicator? Give three specific examples from your work or personal life.

Part 1

Smart Talk
One-On-One

Chapter 1
Discover Your
Own Style

"Do not wish to be anything but what you are,
and try to be that perfectly."

St. Francis De Sales

The first thing you need to recognize is this - *your communication style is unique.* Nurture that uniqueness and use it as a strength to appreciate, rather than a weakness to be overcome.

Ann, a mid-level manager for a media company, had a boss who called her the "voice of reason." He meant she discussed the pros and cons of issues calmly and didn't get carried away in one direction. To him that was a great strength which he depended on. To her it sounded kind of dull. "Sure I do that," she said to herself. "I've always done that." Ann didn't see that quality as a strength because it came naturally to her. In fact, she often wished she could be less level headed. When she listened to some of her fellow managers get in heated arguments with each other, she thought, "I wish I could talk like that. They get everyone's attention. They don't hesitate to say what they think." Like Ann, many of us don't recognize or appreciate our natural communication strengths.

Rather than trying to imitate someone else, *smart talk* key number one is to discover and develop your own unique style of communicating. You can use others as guides and mentors, just as you use this book as a guide, but do not try to become a carbon copy of someone else. You will only become discouraged because, of course, you will never be as good at being that person as they are themselves.

What Is Unique About You?

Start right now to focus on what special qualities you have as a communicator. It could be something as simple as a smile. Mary, a sales representative for a software company, rarely goes anywhere without someone commenting on her winning smile. It is a powerful, non-verbal communication tool for her. It draws people to her. Her smile is her unique calling card.

John, a management consultant, has an appreciative laugh which brightens up any room he's in. Whenever he is present, people feel a little smarter, a little more clever than they usually do. John's laugh is a special communication gift he gives to others.

Carol, an owner of a public relations firm, talks fast. Sometimes people laughingly tell her to slow down, but she shows such energy when she communicates that people like listening to her. She radiates enthusiasm when she talks, and thereby sells her ideas.

Randy, a teacher in a private school, is articulate and introspective. He has a rich speaking voice which he uses deliberately and thoughtfully. When he speaks, he connects with people because he says things they have felt but haven't been able to put into words.

Think about what unique strengths you have as a communicator. Here is a clue as you look. Your strengths will usually be things that you take for granted, things to which you don't pay much attention. That's because they come easily to you. These strengths are a natural extension of yourself.

Use Your Life Experiences

Your experiences are another rich source for discovering what makes you unique. No one else has grown up quite the same as you, or has quite the same genetic make-up. You are one of a kind, and if you learn to share your life experiences in your conversation, you will automatically become unique.

Tom was with a group of friends who were discussing music, and everyone was talking about their favorite artists and groups and what they liked or didn't like about them. Tom finally said, "I really admire all of you. I've never paid much attention to who's singing or what song is playing. I just turn on the radio and listen. How do you connect all those artists and songs and dates in your mind?"

Tom spoke from his life experience. Rather than saying nothing, or pretending to be someone he wasn't, he shared an experience that was different from the others in the group. Revealing your life experiences sometimes takes courage, but it is worth it. It is what makes you original when you talk.

How do you go about discovering your communication style? Ask your friends and co-workers for some feedback. "What is one communication strength you notice in me when we're talking?" Tell them it's for a class assignment (this is your assignment) so you won't feel embarrassed to ask. They might say - "You're a good listener," or, "You tell funny stories," or, "You know so much," etc. Write these comments down on the next page.

Then ask yourself the same question. "What strengths do I have when talking with people one-on-one or in a group?" Write down the strengths you see in yourself on the *Notes to Yourself* page. They may not sound important or powerful to you now, but they will be your strongest asset as you develop your abilities in these next chapters. Discovering what is unique about your style is a key ingredient to becoming the successful communicator you are meant to be.

Summary Chapter 1

Smart Talk Key #1
Appreciate What Is Unique About You
- *Search for your own communication style*
- *Focus on your unique qualities*
- *Draw from your life experiences*
- *Don't try to imitate others*

Notes to Yourself:

List and describe communication strengths others see in you.

List and describe communication strengths you see in yourself.

Notes:

Chapter 2
When You Don't
Know What To Say

"There are two kinds of people in the world:
those who come into a room and say,
"Here I am," and those who come in and say,
"Ah, there you are!""

Anonymous

Have you ever noticed how some people always seem to know just what to say? They put people at ease, they make conversation flow, they are enjoyable to be around. Would you like to be such a person? This chapter is going to tell you how to build that kind of connection with other people.

At work you are constantly building rapport (or tearing it down) with co-workers, clients, vendors, bosses, employees, etc., through your conversations with them. The secret for building rapport is knowing how to start conversations and keep them going.

Starting Conversations

The big secret about starting conversations is that what you say is not nearly as important as you think. Saying something is the key, even if it is just a "Hello" or "Nice day, isn't it?" Being the initiator is your first step in building rapport.

Here is an easy formula for you to use when deciding what to say. In his book, *Conversationally Speaking,* author Alan Garner says you really only have three topics to choose from:

- *the situation*
- *the other person*
- *yourself*

and three ways to begin:

- *asking a question*
- *voicing an opinion*
- *stating a fact*

I like this formula because it's simple and easy to use. Let's apply it to a specific situation. Diane, a marketing analyst for a telecommunications company, is supposed to start training Stan, a new member of their department. Since she is going to be working closely with Stan, she would like to establish rapport with him. Here is how she can use this formula when she gets to the office Monday morning for the first day of training:

Focusing on the Situation
"Hi, Stan. Welcome to our department. I see you've gotten settled at your desk. Don't worry. Your in-basket won't be that empty for long." (*using a fact*)

Focusing on the Other Person
"Hi, Stan. You're in early for a Monday morning. Looks like you beat everyone else in. Are you always a morning person?" (*using a question*)

Focusing on Yourself
"Hi, Stan. Am I glad to be out of that traffic this morning. Makes me wish I could ride my bike rather than my car to work." *(using an opinion)*

By focusing on the situation, the other person, or yourself, you should always be able to come up with material for opening a conversation. And by using a question, an opinion, or a fact, you can engage the other person and begin building rapport.

Keeping Conversations Going

Once you've opened a conversation, how do you keep it going? There are two keys to keeping a conversation from dying (and you along with it):

- Find a Topic of Mutual Interest
- Use Bridges and Transitions

Sometimes you are lucky and the right topic immediately appears. In the example above, after Diane says: "Am I glad to be out of that traffic - makes me wish I could ride my bike rather than my car to work," Stan might respond, "I was riding my bike a lot a couple weeks ago, but not to work. Before starting this job, I took a five day bike tour along the Oregon coast." This conversation is off and running. Biking is a subject they're both excited about.

Using Bridges and Transitions

Sometimes your first topic fails to take off. The other person doesn't respond or has nothing to say about it. Then it's time to use a bridge or transition to a new topic. Just as a bridge connects one shoreline to the other shoreline, a conversational

bridge connects one topic to another.   Here are three
guidelines for using bridges:

- Repeat a Word or Phrase
- Use Connecting Words
- Use Person's Name

1. Repeat a Word or Phrase
Let's look again at Diane's opening to Stan: "Hi, Stan. Am I
glad to be out of that traffic this morning. Makes me wish I
could ride my bike rather than my car to work." Now let's
suppose that Stan is not a biker and doesn't respond to that
topic. Instead he says, "I couldn't get along without my
commute in the morning. *My car* is my refuge. It's the one
time of day when I can be alone with no demands on me."

Notice Stan repeated the phrase *my car* from Diane's
statement and bridged to the topic of being alone with no
demands. Using a phrase from Diane's statement shows
Diane that Stan has listened to her and is responding to what
she said. Now Diane has a chance to bridge to either the
topic of cars or being alone. She chooses to repeat a phrase
Stan used about his car. Diane says, "My car is hardly a
refuge. It's more like a refuse. I have so many McDonald's
bags in there, you'd think I never eat anywhere else but my
car."

Now Stan might decide to bridge to McDonald's. "I know
what you mean. I can't drive past a *McDonald's* without my
kids demanding we stop. Only I make them get out of the car
to eat. Otherwise I'd have more ketchup and mustard on my
upholstery than on their hamburgers."

Do you see how easy it is to repeat a word or phrase from the
last thing that was said? It also has the added benefit of
making the person who just spoke feel you have listened to

them and are responding to what they said, not just waiting for your turn to speak.

2. Use Connecting Words
Connecting words are familiar phrases such as:
"That reminds me of..."
"I know what you mean..."
"Another thing I've noticed is..."
"That is like what happened to me when..."

Stan used *I know what you mean* in his statement above about McDonald's. Diane could reply to Stan's last statement about his kids and McDonald's with, *"That reminds me of* when I let my niece and nephew get a hamburger on the way to the movies last weekend. We ate in the car. What a disaster..."

3. Use Person's Name
Using a person's name is not enough in itself to serve as a bridge, but it can be a nice addition to your connecting words or repetition of a phrase. "I know what you mean, *Diane."* "That reminds me, *Stan*, of the time..." People love to hear their names, and it is a way to personalize your conversation with them.

Using Questions
Asking questions is another way to keep a conversation going. However, be aware that questions can be irritating to the other person if not used appropriately. Here are six guidelines for using questions effectively:

1. Don't Use Yes or No Questions
Unless you are just looking for information, yes and no questions can make the other person feel they are going

through an interrogation rather than carrying on a conversation.

"Are you married?"

"Do you have children?"

"Do you live near here?"

The person will feel as if he or she is filling out a census form, not conversing with someone.

2. Don't Use Leading Questions.

Leading questions make assumptions which may or may not be true. People resent these kinds of questions and will resent you for asking them. Here are some examples of leading questions:

"With your desk such a mess, how to you find anything?"

"Aren't you concerned your department's apathy will reflect on you?"

"Your son's shyness puts him at a disadvantage in sports, doesn't it?"

The person on the receiving end of leading questions is put in a lose/lose situation. If they agree, they feel manipulated. If they disagree, they feel defensive. There is no need to put your conversational partner in that position. Avoid using leading questions.

If you are asked a leading question, always address the assumption, not the question. "Aren't you concerned your *department's apathy* (assumption) will reflect on you?" Your response might be, "My department is actually in good spirits (correcting the assumption). We're making our deadlines without having to work overtime."

3. Don't Change the Subject with Your Question

When asking questions, we often think we are showing interest in the other person and letting them do the talking rather than us. However, if we use our questions to change the subject, we are taking control away from that person, and forcing the conversation in a direction that he or she may not want to go.

Dave and Heather, two co-workers, are talking. Dave says, "I worked so hard all week on that report and I'm afraid my boss isn't even going to read it." Heather asks, "Where is your boss anyway? I've been trying to get a hold of her all day." Heather is changing the subject with her question, and forcing Dave to respond. Not a good way to use a question. She should rather stay with Dave's subject and perhaps ask, "What makes you think your boss won't read it?"

4. Do Use Open Ended Questions

Open-ended questions are those that can't be answered by a yes or no.

Closed: "Did you like the movie?"
Open: "What did you like about the movie?"
Closed: "Will you have that report done today?"
Open: "How are you coming on that report?"
Closed: "Do you work out?"
Open: "What do you like to do to work out?"

Open-ended questions encourage the other person to use more than a one or two word answer. They give the conversation a better chance of succeeding. Other open-ended phrases that help build a conversation are "Tell me about that," or "Describe that for me."

5. Do Use Who, What When, Where, Why

These are called the five W's, and every journalism student is taught to answer them when they write a story. In conversations, these words encourage the speaker to elaborate on what he or she is saying. They show you are interested and want to hear more. You saw examples of the five W's in the previous examples of open-ended questions. An easy way to make sure you are using open-ended, rather than close-ended questions, is to start with the words who, what, when, where, or why.

6. Do Turn Your Question Into a Statement
To prevent your questions from taking over the direction of the conversation, try making statements that reflect what the person is saying rather than asking a question. When Dave says, "I worked so hard all week on that report and I'm afraid my boss isn't even going to read it," instead of responding with a question, Heather could make a statement. "I saw how hard you were working on that report." That keeps Dave in control of the conversation, and shows him Heather is empathetic to his situation. Then he is free to continue his thoughts on the subject.

Keeping a conversation going is easy when you use bridges, transitions, and questions. Your goal is to find common ground on which you can build rapport. When you do that, you are on your way to enjoying your conversations, and the person with whom you are conversing will enjoy them too.

Summary for Chapter 2

Smart Talk Key #2
Find Common Ground To Build Rapport
- *Use the situation, other person, or yourself for conversation starters*
- *Use bridges and transitions to continue the conversation*
- *Don't use questions to change the subject*

Notes to Yourself:

List three conversation openers you used this week and describe how the other person responded.

List three bridges or transitions you used in conversations this week.

List three open-ended questions you used in conversations this week and the responses you got.

Notes:

Chapter 3
An Easy Way To Handle the Difficult

"If the only tool you have is a hammer, you tend to see every problem as a nail."

Abraham Maslow

In chapter two we looked at ways to establish rapport with people. We learned some easy techniques for starting conversations and keeping them going. This ability to connect with others is essential for your business and personal success. However, there are times when building rapport isn't enough. We all run into difficult situations when we come face to face with a conflict between ourselves and another person. It may be a disagreement with a co-worker, employee, family member, or friend. How do we handle such conflict with finesse? Here are two techniques that will help you:

- Find a Point of Agreement
- Talk in Terms of the Problem

Find a Point of Agreement

Salespeople have known this secret for years. When they are faced with difficult buyers who throw up objections to their product, they are taught to agree with the buyer.

Buyer: "Your pricing isn't competitive. I can get this product cheaper elsewhere."

Salesperson: (finds point of agreement) "Price is important in any buying decision. Our price is slightly above some of our competitors because..."

Notice how this response puts the salesperson on the side of the buyer. If the salesperson had said, "Buying based only on price is a risky business practice," it would put him/her in an adversarial relationship with the customer. That is not where a salesperson wants to be.

Steve, a financial manager for an outdoor advertising company, used the agreement technique when he had to answer his boss's irate questions about the incorrect sales forecasts his department had produced.

Boss: "How can we run this business without accurate sales forecasts to work from?"

Steve: "(finds point of agreement) "I know how important these sales forecasts are to our operation. I'm talking with our software supplier now to find out why these errors are occurring, and how we can correct them."

Compare this to the response that Steve could have made. "My department is doing the best we can. There is an error in our computer system and they haven't been able to tell me what it is yet." Notice how this response puts Steve in a defensive position, instead of on his boss's side.

Finding a point of agreement can also be used when the criticism is aimed at you personally. Nobody likes to be criticized. Whether it is justified or not, criticism hurts, especially when it questions our competency. When you are facing personal criticism, find a point of agreement. It will help you maintain your dignity and at the same time reduce the friction between the two of you.

Laura was the president of a community organization. Attendance at their bi-monthly meetings had been leveling off, even dropping in the last few months. At a board meeting, John, one of the group's officers, stood up and said, "Our membership is falling and so is the quality of our meetings. The president needs to provide leadership to uphold this organization, and I don't think you're doing that, Laura."

How was Laura to respond? Here she was, being criticized, not in private, but in front of her fellow officers, people whose respect she valued. Laura could respond in one of two ways. She could disagree with what John had said and defend her performance and the organization's performance. She might say, "I think your accusations are unfair and inaccurate. If it hadn't been for my efforts, this organization would be in worse shape than it is now. If officers such as yourself would show more support, we could be more successful." How likely is it that Laura would gain John's cooperation with a response like that?

The other option would be for Laura to find a point of agreement with what John said, and still keep her dignity. That is not as tough as it sounds. Here is a response Laura could have made:

. "John, I appreciate your concerns about our membership numbers and the quality of our meetings (finds point of agreement). Both these issues are at the core of our group's success.   As president of this organization, I am committed to membership growth and quality meetings.   They are both on the agenda for today.   On the issue of leadership, let's get together after the meeting and discuss that further."

Notice how this response keeps the situation from escalating, and leaves an opportunity for Laura and John to continue a working relationship with each other.   That's the power of looking for a point of agreement.

Another technique is to use the *feel, felt, found* formula.   With this approach, you empathize with the other person's feelings, while at the same time offering another point of view. Suppose you are a parent arguing with your daughter about practicing her music lesson.

Daughter: "I hate practicing the flute.   It's too hard.   I want to go over to my friend's house."
Parent: "I understand how you *feel.*   I often *felt* that way when I was practicing the French horn growing up.   What I *found* is that knowing how to play an instrument opened so many doors for me.   I even met my first boyfriend playing in band."

You can also use the *feel, felt, found* formula in terms of *they* rather than *I.*   Suppose a new employee is protesting having to turn in a weekly progress report.

Employee: "These weekly reports are a waste of time for me. I could get more done and get out of here on time if I didn't have to fill them out.
Employer: "I understand how you *feel.*   Many employees in your position have *felt* that way at first.   What they've *found* after doing them for a couple months is that they are a helpful track record.   They can see the steps they've taken to accomplish a project, and evaluate which ones have paid off."

The important thing to remember is that when you are facing a conflict or disagreement, you don't want to start out defending yourself or attacking the other person. Instead, you want to look for that point of agreement. Then you will be setting yourself up for success rather than failure.

Talk in Terms of the Problem

The next crucial step for handling conflict is to talk in terms of the problem, not the person. Instead of personalizing the conflict, keep focused on the issue. In her book, *A Woman's Guide to the Language of Success,* author Phyllis Mindell, Ph.D., recommends choosing words which distance yourself from the personal (you or the other person).

Let's see how this works. Catherine, an office manager for a law firm, had an employee who was consistently arriving late for work. She knew the other employees resented this, and she needed to say something to Greg about his lateness. Here are three ways she could address Greg:

In terms of herself: "*I need* you to arrive here by 8:00 a.m. from now on. *I can't* have the rest of the staff resenting your being late.

In terms of the other person: "*You've been* late every day this week. *You are* causing resentment among the rest of the staff."

In terms of the problem: "*Being late* disrupts the work flow and causes resentment among the rest of the staff. Please *arrive on time* from now on."

Speaking in terms of the problem minimizes the conflict between the two people. It focuses attention on the issue, where it should be, and decreases the likelihood of the conflict escalating to the personal plane where unnecessary accusations might fly back and forth.

Catherine used this technique outside of work when she addressed a conflict between her and her ski partner, Jeff. They were well matched in terms of skiing ability and usually had great fun together. But now the spring snow was heavy and wet, and it was difficult to ski. Jeff's remedy was to ski through it as fast as possible. Catherine, who didn't feel comfortable skiing that fast, was left far behind, and it made skiing together less enjoyable than usual. Catherine could approach the subject in three ways:

In terms of herself: "*I can't* keep up with you in this kind of snow. It's no fun *for me* to try to ski at this pace."
In terms of the other person: "*You* are skiing too fast. Why can't you slow down a little? *You're* a hazard to other skiers."
In terms of the problem: "This *heavy, spring snow* is difficult to maneuver in. *Skiing slower* would allow more time to execute turns."

She chose the last option, and that opened up a discussion which allowed them to compromise on their skiing speed. The result was an enjoyable skiing day for both of them, rather than a fight neither of them wanted.

All of us will face occasional conflicts when we communicate with others. How we handle those disagreements will do much to determine our satisfaction with our professional and personal lives. Use the techniques in this chapter to make your difficult situations easier to handle.

Summary for Chapter 3

Smart Talk Key #3
Focus On the Problem, Not the Person

- *Find a point of agreement*
- *Distance yourself from the personal*
- *Talk in terms of the problem*

Notes To Yourself:

Describe a conversation you had this week when you looked for a point of agreement. What did you say and how did the other person respond?

Describe a situation this week when you used the *"feel, felt, found"* technique. What were the results?

Describe a conversation this week when you addressed the problem, rather than the other person or yourself. What were the results?

Chapter 4
When in Doubt,
Do This

Explanation given by a pupil for not talking:
"I think I'll learn more by listening. Anything
I would say I already know."

Quoted by The Christian Science Monitor

Susan is often told by people that she is a good listener. She has never appreciated that compliment, because she interprets it to mean that she is quiet and doesn't speak up in conversations. "You don't get ahead in the business world by being quiet," she says. "I want to be noticed. I want people to think of me as someone who *speaks* well, not someone who *listens* well."

Many people view the communication process the same way Susan does. They think speaking is the important thing. Listening is something you do until it's your turn to talk. If communication were just a one way process, Susan's view might be valid. The better you speak the better communicator you are. But of course that is only half the picture.

Unless you enjoy talking to yourself, the whole idea of communication is to share information, ideas, and feelings with another person. And in turn, that person shares their information, ideas and feelings with you. If neither party is interested in listening to the other person, communication is not going to take place. Listening is key for your success.

Always Have a Purpose for Listening

The secret to being a good listener is simple. Have a reason for listening. If you don't know why you are listening, you will soon stop. Your mind will wander, you will be distracted, and you won't concentrate on what the other person is saying. Why should you? You haven't given your mind a reason to listen. If you have a purpose for listening, you will tune in.

Sometimes that purpose is easy to identify. Suppose you are getting directions to your travel agency to pick up tickets for your upcoming vacation. You want to get those directions down right. Perhaps you even ask the travel agent to repeat what she said to make sure you heard her correctly. You are motivated to listen because you are excited to pick up those tickets.

Finding a purpose for listening is not always that easy. Sometimes we are talking with people who we think are boring, unclear, or have nothing to say. Sometimes we disagree with what they are saying or are intimidated by them. In these situations, finding a purpose for listening becomes a creative act on our part. The goal is to always identify a purpose that matters to you and motivates you to listen.

Listening When You Don't Want To

Jim had an employee in his department who talked on and on. Asking this person, "How was your weekend?," was dangerous because he got a blow by blow of everything that occurred from Friday afternoon to Monday morning. He tuned out soon after her description of what she cooked for dinner Friday night.

Jim did not want to avoid talking to this employee. She was a good worker and an asset to the department. He needed a reason for listening to her. He decided his purpose was to make her feel a valuable part of the team - not just for the work she did but for the person she was. That purpose motivated him to listen to her.

He also decided to put parameters around his listening time. He would give her a few minutes in the morning, and then excuse himself for a telephone call, a meeting, etc. That way he would not be pretending to listen long after he had tuned out, and he would be setting an example of an appropriate time limit for discussions of this kind to the rest of his staff.

Listening When You Disagree

Barbara, a financial manager for an investment firm, had trouble listening to Allen, the marketing manager of her company. He always seemed to have the opposite opinion of hers. She often became impatient and angry when he talked, and found herself wanting to interrupt and defend herself and her ideas.

Barbara realized she didn't have a positive motivation for listening to Allen. The next time they talked, she decided to stop thinking about disagreeing and contradicting what he said. Instead, she simply listened to understand his viewpoint.

After he finished speaking, she said, "Let me think about what you've said, and I'll get back to you with my thoughts this afternoon." She allowed herself the freedom to listen for understanding only, without feeling pressure to respond at that moment. Narrowing her purpose enabled her to listen rather than react to the marketing director's views, even when they were in opposition to her own.

What If You Want To Listen But They Don't Want To Talk
Sometimes you are ready and willing to listen, but the other person has difficulty talking. They may be shy, they may have trouble expressing themselves, or they may be afraid to talk to you.

Brian wanted to mentor a new employee in his department who was very quiet. Several times he tried to engage him in conversation, but Brian would end up doing all the talking. He wondered, "What do you do when you want to listen, but they won't talk?"

This is when your listening skills become even more important. You want to give the person every opportunity to talk without their feeling manipulated or forced into talking. Here are three tips for handling reluctant talkers:

1. Slow Down
Our first reaction is to talk faster and say more to compensate for the lack of response from the other person. Instead, take a breath, relax, and just feel content to be with that other person.

2. Be Comfortable with Silence
Often times the other person will respond if we give them a little time. But if we jump in as soon as there is a moment of silence, we don't allow that person a chance to speak up.

3. Try Short Conversations at First
Don't go for long conversations at the beginning. A few exchanged words is plenty. Build from there. Use the following approach. Take one conversational step forward. If they respond, take another step. If they don't, take one step back, and look for another opportunity.

As we said at the beginning of this chapter, communication is a two way process. When Susan said, "I want people to think of me as someone who *speaks* well, not someone who *listens* well," she was not appreciating the full magic of the communication process. Being adept at both speaking and listening will make you a more valuable person in your workplace. People will seek you out and want to talk with you.

Summary for Chapter 4

Smart Talk Key #4
Listen

- *Recognize that listening is as important as speaking*
- *Have a purpose for listening*
- *Slow down*
- *Don't be afraid of silence*

Notes To Yourself:

Describe two listening opportunities you took advantage of this week. Identify the purpose for your listening in each case.

Describe how you slowed down, used silence, and tried short conversations to allow a reluctant talker to express themselves.

Part 2

Smart Talk
In Groups

Chapter 5
When Someone Else Has The Floor

*"The greatest good you can do for another
is not just to share your riches
but to reveal to him his own."*

Benjamin Disraeli

Now that you have the basic techniques for talking one-on-one, we are ready to move on to the challenge of talking in small groups. As soon as there are more than two of you together, you will find a whole new set of communication dynamics takes over. Whether you are sitting around a conference table with a group of business associates, or around a restaurant table with family and friends, if you don't understand how group communication works, you will often feel unsure and unable to contribute effectively.

How Does Group Communication Work?

Don't feel bad if you can't answer that question. You are not alone. Many people do not understand how it works, and the quality of most of our group communication reflects that lack of knowledge. Just think back to all the group meetings or gatherings in which you have participated. Do one of these things often happen?

- One person dominates the conversation and no one else gets a word in.
- Everyone is trying to talk at the same time and no one is listening.
- No one can think of anything to say, and there are awkward silences.

These are all examples of poor group communication, and they happen so often that many people think that's just the way things are. This doesn't have to be the case. The key to good group communication is to follow the rules for what Suzette Elgin, Ph.D., author of *Genderspeak,* calls topics and turns. The next three chapters will apply the rules for topics and turns to your group communication challenges.

Show Support for Each Others' Topics

Showing support for others may sound like common sense, but it is not often common practice. Have you ever been in a meeting where you have finally gotten up your nerve to make a point, but when you do, everyone ignores it as if you had never spoken, or they immediately dismiss it as irrelevant and move on to something else? Being ignored, rather than supported by the rest of the group, hurts the individual and it hurts the communication process.

An easy way to support others' topics is through non-verbal communication. Simply show the person speaking that you are listening to what they are saying. *Show* is the key word here. If you don't demonstrate any of the non-verbal feedback listed below, the speaker won't know you are listening, even if you are. He or she won't feel any support from you and may actually assume you are not listening. You don't want that to happen.

Use these Four Non-Verbal Appreciation Cues

1. *Look At Them.*

How disconcerting it is for a speaker to see that the eyes of the group are not focused on them. He or she immediately assumes the group is not listening to what they are saying. If you are looking at your day planner or at someone else in the group, you are unconsciously signaling to the speaker that you don't think they are important enough for you to listen to them. You don't want to send that signal. Make a habit of giving the speaker your eye contact. You will be amazed how often he or she will begin to address you as a key member of the group.

2. *Nod Your Head*

A nod of your head is a non-verbal way to convey understanding to the speaker. It doesn't necessarily mean agreement. It simply means, "I understand, I'm following what you're saying, I'm with you." Every speaker will appreciate that kind of support.

3. *Keep Your Facial Expression Alive*

A speaker who sees a deadpan face in the group sees an uninterested face. I remember once cutting my remarks short because the faces in the group were so expressionless. I thought they were totally disinterested. Later they told me, "No, we wanted to hear what you were saying."

To keep from sending the wrong message to the speaker, respond with facial expressions. Show surprise, amusement, agreement, puzzlement, etc. You can do that with an arch of the eyebrows, a smile, widening the eyes, furrowing your brow, opening your mouth, etc. Keeping your face alive tells the speaker you are listening and responding.

4. Chuckle or Laugh
We all know how good it feels to get an appreciative laugh from an audience. It is music to a speaker's ears. Gretchen performs with an improvisation group. She says, "Applause is great, but when the audience *laughs*, that's when we know we've connected. There's no feeling like it." When a group responds to us with an appreciative laugh or chuckle, we feel they are not only listening to us, but that they like us too.

I realize what a powerful feedback tool a chuckle can be every time I talk to my brother on the phone. We live 1000 miles apart so I call him every Sunday. He lost his ability to speak several years ago. It's slowly coming back but it is still difficult for him to converse. Yet he never lost his chuckle. When we talk each week, he uses that chuckle many times in response to what I say. He makes me feel I'm the most clever and entertaining person around. And he does it without saying a word.

When I walk down the hallways of businesses, listening to group conversations, I notice the person who has an appreciative laugh energizes the group, and people like to have them around. So experiment in private to find a comfortable chuckle that feels right for you, and then start using it in public. You will be amazed at the response. And you will also be amazed at how much more connected to the group you will feel.

How To Support Topics Verbally

Once you have used these non-verbal techniques to support the speaker, you can add some verbal responses. An easy way to start is by using the speaker's name and encouraging them to continue.

"That's interesting, Dan. Please go on."
"That's a good point, Dan."
"Yes, Dan, I agree."

You can also add a question which encourages Dan to continue:

"That's interesting, Dan. What do you think will happen...?"
"That's a good point, Dan. How do you think people will react...?"
"Yes, Dan, I agree. Who do you think could help with...?

If you want to add something to Dan's topic, connect your comment to something he said by repeating a phrase he used. "I agree with Dan that our customer base is shrinking. One way to turn that around would be..."

If you want to add something to Dan's topic and you do not agree with what he has been saying, don't contradict or refute his statements. Instead, look for a way to acknowledge his comments and then offer your opinion. "Dan sees our customer base shrinking because he is comparing the number of customers this year to last year. Another way to look at it is to compare sales volume this year to last year..."

Supporting the speaker's topic does not mean always agreeing. It simply means honoring their right to be a valuable contributor to the group. Nothing will be more appreciated by others than your show of support for them when they are speaking. The important key here is *show*.

Don't assume they know. Let them see and hear your support. When you do, you will fast become a welcome and effective member of any group.

Summary Chapter 5

Smart Talk Key #5
Show Support For Each Others' Topics

- *Look at the speaker*
- *Nod your head*
- *Laugh or chuckle*
- *Ask speaker to continue*
- *Avoid a deadpan facial expression*
- *Don't contradict the speaker*

Notes to Yourself:

In private, experiment to find a chuckle that feels right for you. Watch a TV comedy, a funny movie, or read the comics. Practice laughing out loud until you find a comfortable, non-offensive chuckle. Then try using it in public. Write down the results.

Use the non-verbal feedback techniques we discussed (eye contact, nodding, facial expressions) at your next meeting or group gathering. Write down where and how you used them. Also write down how the speaker responded.

Use the verbal feedback techniques we discussed ("that's a good point, please go on, another way of looking at this") at your next meeting or group gathering. Write down where and how you used them. Also write down how the speaker responded.

Notes:

Chapter 6
Who Gets The Floor

*"We find comfort among those who agree with us -
growth among those who don't."*

Frank A. Clark

Taking turns is the next key for communicating in small groups. Sounds obvious, doesn't it? Didn't we learn that clear back in kindergarten? Everyone gets to play, everyone gets their turn. No one should grab someone else's turn, no one should take all the turns for themselves, and no one should have to sit on the sidelines and never get a turn.

It appears to be common courtesy, but how many times have you seen these courtesies violated in your group conversations? I would guess the majority of time. It is not that everyone becomes rude and inconsiderate as soon as they join a group conversation. More often it is just that they don't know how the rules for taking turns work when it comes to communicating in groups. Don't put yourself in that category. Learn and follow these four simple guidelines for taking turns:

1. Don't Interrupt

Most of us know better than to interrupt, but we do it anyway. We've all heard people interrupt the speaker with remarks such as:

"Wait, Larry, I just had an idea."

"That's unrealistic, Larry. We don't have the budget for that."

"Larry, we've tried that before. It doesn't work."

That is not how we want our group conversations to run. We want each person who is speaking to finish their thought and come to a natural stopping point before anyone else begins to speak.

2. Let the Current Speaker Choose the Next Speaker

The group should follow the lead of the current speaker. That person has the right to decide who gets to speak next. Here is how powerful this rule can be when you practice it. Suppose you are the current speaker, and you are concerned that Tony has not had a chance to contribute to the meeting. Perhaps you know he is a bit intimidated about speaking up in this group. You could make it easier for him by selecting him as the next speaker.

"Tony, you've had a lot of experience in this area, what are some of your thoughts?" or,

"Tony, what do you see that we have not yet addressed?"

You have just expanded participation within the group and that is a key ingredient for effective group communication.

Or let's say you want the group to adopt your recommendation on an issue. You have just stated your views and you'd like the group to hear some additional support for your proposal before anyone speaks against it. You can

choose someone as the next speaker who shares your
viewpoint. "Nancy, you've done a lot of work on this issue.
Could you share with the group what you've found?"

The same thing works in a social situation. If you are afraid
Art is going to start speaking again as soon as you are
through (he's been monopolizing the conversation all
evening), choose someone else to be the speaker after you.
"Ted, I know you've had better luck than I shopping on-line.
What works for you?" If all group participants used their
power to select the next speaker, there would be much less
chance for one person to dominate the conversation.

3. Don't Keep a Turn Too Long
What is too long? That depends a lot on the situation. Three
to six sentences is the norm. However, if you are discussing a
complicated issue in a meeting, each person's turn may take
awhile. Be considerate and warn the group when your turn is
going to take longer than usual. Give them a guideline so they
will know where you are going with your comments.
"I have three points I want to make about this issue."
"There are two factors that concern me about this proposal."
Then make your points as briefly as you can.

If you are telling a story, either to make a point in a meeting,
or to entertain at a social gathering, be conscious of an
appropriate length. We have all been on the receiving end
of narratives which seem to never end. The whole group
suffers, and your story suffers too.

Keep it brief. The way to do that is to focus on the point of
the story without adding detail that is unnecessary. If you are
telling a story about sliding off the road when driving over a
snowy mountain pass, you don't have to describe for us the
mountain scenery or where you stopped for lunch. Include
only the details that are pertinent to the point of your story -

the weather, the road conditions, who was in the car with you, etc. You will keep the group's interest that way and not monopolize the conversation.

4. Each Person Gets an Equal Number of Turns

The final guideline for taking turns is to let each person in the group have an equal number of turns. I know you do not have total control of this since you are just one person in the group, but you can do your part to make sure this happens. If you find yourself doing most of the talking, back off and let others have a chance.

On the other hand, if you haven't contributed anything, look for an opportunity to speak. I attended a meeting once when the leader of the group said, "All right, now we're going to hear from anyone who has not yet spoken." I was embarrassed to realize I was one of the two or three to which he was referring. I had no good reason for not having contributed up to that point. I was just being too cautious or too lazy. As a member of a group, consider it both a right and a responsibility to speak up.

If you are the leader of a group, be aware that how you structure a group discussion will influence the number of turns each person takes. In her book *Talking from 9 to 5,* Deborah Tannen, Ph.D., professor of linguistics, says that in open discussions where speakers have to get the floor for themselves in order to speak, less forceful participants tend to say less and initiate less. When the opportunity to speak is handed to these same participants, in other words, when they are *given* a turn instead of *fighting* for a turn, they contribute more equally. This is something to keep in mind when you are structuring your meetings.

Letting each person have a turn to speak applies to social situations as well. Marsha used this rule when she was invited to her corporate headquarters to be honored along with other top performers within her company.

At a group dinner that night, she said, "Why don't we go around the table and each of us tell our life story in five minutes or less?" The group agreed, and they had a lively discussion with everyone participating. If she had not proposed giving each person a turn, I am sure there would have been some who would have hung back and not participated. When you hand someone a turn, never force that person to contribute. But offering them a chance will usually increase the likelihood of their speaking up.

By using these rules, you can be a catalyst in groups to encourage everyone to take their turn, and to keep anyone from monopolizing all the turns. When you do that, you will make your meetings more effective and your social gatherings more fun. And you will become an important and welcome addition to any group.

Summary for Chapter 6

Smart Talk Key #6
Give Everyone a Turn To Speak
- *Let the current speaker choose the next speaker*
- *Give each person an equal number of turns*
- *Hand people their turn when appropriate*
- *Don't interrupt*
- *Don't keep a turn too long*

Notes to Yourself:

Apply these five rules for taking turns in your up-coming group conversations or meetings. Write down who the group was and how you applied these rules. Describe the results.

Chapter 7
How To Take the Floor

*"Since you are writing the script
of your life, make it a starring role."*

Anonymous

In chapter five you learned how to show support for topics
that others introduce, and in chapter six, how to take turns
when speaking. There is one more thing you need to know to
be a successful group communicator - how to take the floor
and introduce your own topics.

Speaking up and introducing a subject is a little scarier than
listening and responding, because now you are moving from
the background to the foreground. When you introduce a new
direction for the group discussion, you are taking the lead,
and putting yourself in the spotlight. In some groups, this
step can be intimidating. Don't let your fears stop you,
however. Remember, this isn't like rock climbing, where one
wrong step can mean death. This is a lot more like baseball,

where the best batters are also the ones who strike out the most. As Mickey Mantle said, when he was responding to critics who pointed out that he struck out 1,710 times in his career: "They may be strikeouts to some people, but to me, every one of them was nearly a home run."

Introducing topics is something you can try and fail and still survive. In fact, the people who have success are the ones who do it the most. We are going to look at four techniques that will help you hit a home run when you introduce your topics:

- Speak Up Early
- Prepare Your Point and Example
- Know How To Tell Stories
- Pick Topics That Interest You

1. Speak Up Early

Putting things off never makes it any easier, and in group communication, it actually makes it harder. If you keep waiting for the ideal time to bring up your point, the group will get in the habit of carrying on their conversation without you. They won't be expecting you to contribute. Then if you finally bring something up at the last minute, they will regard it as out of place and an intrusion on their conversation.

Another advantage of speaking up early is that even if you don't bring anything else up the rest of the time, people will think of you as a contributor. If you say something at the beginning of the meeting, you will get credit for it throughout the meeting, whether you say anything more or not. If you say the same thing at the end, you will get much less credit. So look for an opportunity to speak up early in a group. It will pay off for you.

2. Prepare Your Point with an Example

Especially in business meetings, start out with your point so people immediately know what you are going to talk about. Phil, a business manager for a TV station, was in a managers' meeting and wanted to bring up the issue of a new phone system. The current discussion regarding quarterly advertising plans was winding down. He connected his topic to the previous one and made his primary point:

"Another thing we wanted to look at this quarter was the purchase of a new phone system. It's a big investment, and just like our advertising plan, it's important we make a decision to go forward and invest in up-to-date technology." Notice how Phil used words from the previous topic - *quarter, advertising plan* - and made a smooth transition to his topic, a new phone system. He stated his point up front - we should go forward and purchase an up to date system.

Phil has made a good start, but he doesn't want to leave his point there. Backing up his point with an example will give the rest of the group a reason for looking at his proposal. Phil continues:

"Our salespeople are frustrated because they can't receive more than one call at a time with our current system. Last week, Cindy, one of our top performers, was waiting for a callback confirmation regarding a big advertising order, and because our phone system couldn't let her know she had a call waiting when she was on the phone, she missed the call and almost missed the order. We can't afford to risk losing sales because of our out-dated technology. I recommend we move on this purchase now."

Phil has introduced his point, given an example, and repeated his point. Now the rest of the group can respond.

3. Know How To Tell Stories

When you are talking casually with a group of people, stories are a popular communication tool. They are easy for the group to follow, they're entertaining, and they can be used to illustrate a point. I am not talking about jokes and canned stories. Those grow stale very quickly, and nothing is less anticlimactic than telling a story people have already heard. I am talking about real stories from your life.

If you are not comfortable telling stories, it is an important skill for you to master. After the business meeting or seminar, when everyone gathers for lunch, dinner or a drink to relax and talk non-business, stories will be the chief vehicle for conversation. No matter how much you contributed during the meetings, if you can't join in the informal conversations afterwards, you will be at a big disadvantage. Your boss and co-workers will often see you as stiff or withdrawn and not very fun to be around. They will trust you less, because they won't feel they know you.

If you are not used to telling stories, it may seem intimidating right now, but don't worry. Here are four simple tips to help you:

- Have a Point To Your Story
- Play Yourself Down, Not Up
- Have a Beginning, Middle, and End
- Leave Out Unnecessary Detail

a) Have a Point To Your Story

Having a point is a nice safety net when you're unsure of your story's entertainment value. Even if the group doesn't respond with the laughter you had hoped, if there is a point to your story, you won't suffer the embarrassment that you might otherwise. There is still a legitimate reason for telling

your anecdote. Your point doesn't have to be profound. If
you were telling a story about your first golf experience, your
point could be - " I found out golf was not going to be my
game."

b) Play Yourself Down, Not Up
If you are a good golfer, you wouldn't choose the story about
your incredible winning streak last summer. Somehow stories
of mistakes, errors, and upsets go over better than victories,
trophies and standing ovations. As Garrison Keillor,
consummate story-teller and host of his radio show "Prairie
Home Companion," says: "Sunny days do not make good
stories."

When you choose a story from your life, pick one that puts
you in a vulnerable, funny or threatening position. The group
will appreciate it more. Telling a story about your successes
sounds too much like bragging. If you're a good golfer, tell
about the time you landed in the sand trap, not when you had
a perfect score.

And don't play the "I can top that" game with your stories.
Even if you have climbed higher, traveled farther or run faster
than the last person, don't downplay their anecdote with a
more spectacular one of your own. Express appreciation for
their story and then tell yours in a way that does not detract
from theirs.

c) Have a Beginning, Middle, and End
If you've ever written a story, you know the plot must have a
beginning, middle and end. The same thing should be true of
the stories you tell. It will keep your anecdote moving and
keep the interest of the group.
• The beginning should set the scene
• The middle should build to a climax
• The end should wrap it up

If I were going to tell a story about a back-packing experience, I would structure it this way:

Beginning: Who, when, where
A few years ago my cousin, brother and I took a backpack trip in the Sangre de Cristo mountains.

Middle: Build suspense to climax
I had to start out a day later than they did, so I took my dog for company. I was supposed to meet them at Willow Lake. It was a hard climb and I didn't make it up to the lake until almost nightfall. When I finally arrived, no one was there. I hadn't brought food or a tent, so I didn't want to stay up there alone. I was tired, but I told my dog CJ, "We're going back down." I couldn't see the trail because it was totally dark by now. But CJ acted like he knew where to go, so I put him on his leash, held on to the other end, and followed him. Climbing over rocks, shrubs, brush and water, with no trail in sight, CJ got us all the way down the mountain in the dark.

End: Wrap it up
If it hadn't been for my dog, I wouldn't have gotten down that mountain by myself. I credit CJ for saving my life, or at least saving me from a very miserable night.

d) Leave Out Unnecessary Detail
Be careful that you don't digress from your story with unnecessary detail or side paths. Don't do this:
A few years ago my cousin, brother and I took a backpack trip in the Sangre de Cristo mountains. *My cousin lived in Dallas, my brother in Minnesota, so it was a long trip for them to get here.* (Unnecessary detail). *One year my brother never did make it because he got sick right before he was to fly out.* (Unnecessary digression). Keep your story to the point. Your audience will appreciate it.

Story telling is an important skill for you to practice. One of America's greatest presidents, Abraham Lincoln, made almost all his points with stories. Cultivate that ability yourself, and you will have a valuable tool for taking the floor and getting peoples' attention.

4. *Introduce Topics That Interest You*

When you are in more informal group situations, where the range of topics open for discussion is broader than in structured meetings, you need to be prepared to bring up subjects to talk about. You will never be successful introducing a topic if you are not interested in it yourself. That means you have to cultivate interests that will be exciting for you to discuss.

- Those interests might be sports or recreational activities you enjoy. Do you bike, ski, golf, garden, camp, hike?
- They might be arts and cultural pursuits. Do you play an instrument, paint, dance, attend the symphony, theater, movies?
- You might be active in organizations. Do you work for a political party, volunteer for a hospice, help out at your children's school, support environmental causes?
- How about educational pursuits? Are you taking any classes, working for a degree, taking an investment course, a computer class, a public speaking class?
- What are you reading - the local newspaper, the Wall Street Journal, Time, Forbes, books, the internet?

You can see the range of topics for you to introduce is endless. The key to your success is having a genuine interest in the subjects you choose. Your enthusiasm for the topic will then carry you through your initial fears of speaking up.

Taking the floor and introducing topics in a group can be exhilarating. It can also sometimes be intimidating. Don't let fear stop you. Follow the techniques in this chapter and step up to bat.   Remember Mickey Mantle's attitude - every hit you take is a potential home run. As we said at the beginning of this chapter, you are the only one who is writing the script for your life. So by all means, give yourself a starring role.

Summary for Chapter 7

Smart Talk Key #7
Step Into the Spotlight

- *Speak up early*
- *Prepare your point and example*
- *Know how to tell stories*
- *Introduce topics you are excited about*

Notes to Yourself:

Prepare a point and example for your next business meeting.
Write down the results.

Put together a story from your life with a beginning, middle
and end. Write down the main points.

List five topics you are interested in and could introduce in a
group. Use one and write down the results.

Notes:

Chapter 8
Life Is A Stage

"All the world's a stage, and all the men and women merely players. They have their exits and their entrances. And one man in his time plays many parts."

Shakespeare

We all take on many different roles in a typical day. We might be mother or father in the morning, boss or employee at work, accountant or salesperson on the job, hockey player or committee member after work, spouse or significant other in the evening.

When communicating in a group, you will also be taking on various roles. The more you know about what roles are out there and what the characteristics of those roles are, the more successful you will be participating in a group.

People Want the Spotlight
First, be aware that whenever there are more than two people together, they will become self-conscious and often compete for the spotlight. Each person wants the group's attention on them. They do not want to be ignored or left out. You will feel this way yourself. It is just human nature. Don't take this competing for position too seriously. If you constantly worry about who is in the spotlight and who isn't, you will not enjoy the conversation at all. And if you never find a comfortable role for yourself in the group, you won't contribute as much as you could.

Ron, an IT director for an electronics firm, was in that dilemma. He used to dread the staff meetings with his fellow management team. He never knew what to say. He would listen to the sales manager and marketing director boasting about their upcoming plans, and he would think, "How can I compete with that?"

Ron was asking himself the wrong question. He doesn't have to compete with the sales and marketing managers' roles. That's a losing proposition for him. He needs to develop a role for himself based on his talents and personality. We are going to look at some of the roles Ron might choose for himself. But first the following point needs to be emphasized:

The Leader Is Not the Only Role
Most of us think there is only one important role in a group, and that is the leader. The assumption is if you're the leader, you get to run the show. If you are not, you fade into the background. The leader will get the credit and the spotlight. That is why there is often much jockeying for the leadership position. But these assumptions are not accurate.

Roles Besides the Leader
There are so many other roles to play in a group besides the
leader that will still get you recognized. Here are just a few
listed by author Fran Rees, in her book *Teamwork from Start
to Finish.*
Suggestion maker:
Offers suggestions as to how to proceed to get the problem
solved.
Summarizer:
Summarizes what has been covered
Information Seeker:
Asks for facts, opinions, feelings and alternatives
Topic Guardian:
Keeps the group from going off on tangents
Gate Keeper:
Brings others into the discussion
Clarifier:
Helps others clarify their ideas
Harmonizer:
Smoothes over the team's rough spots
Humorist:
Relieves tension
Includer:
Draws in team members who are quiet
Gate closer:
Closes discussion on an issue
Devil's Advocate:
Identifies holes in the team's thinking.

And you don't have to be restricted to just these roles. You
can make up your own role to fit your talents and the group
you are in.

Chris was on the board of a community organization. He
hesitated speaking up at their business meetings because they
were required to use strict *Robert's Rules of Order*, and he

thought the rules were cumbersome and time consuming. He knew his role would not be that of parliamentarian!

However, Chris did want to contribute to this group, so he sought a role for himself. As he listened, he heard them talking about the need for someone to be in charge of calling back people who had inquired about their organization. He thought, "I believe in that, and I could organize it." So he volunteered to take on that task, and now he has a role and something of value to say when he reports back to the group at their meetings.

Teri wanted to contribute to her small ranching community but didn't want to take on an elected position on the town council. She was an avid gardener. She thought - "I could take on the role of providing flowers for all the public places in town - the park, the main street, etc." Each spring she now starts and plants hundreds of flowers for her town. She took on a role which is easy for her to talk about because she believes in what she is doing.

Taking on a role works in social groups as well. How many times have you not spoken up because you couldn't seem to find a role for yourself in the group? You felt superfluous and perhaps ignored. Here again, create a role! Does the group need someone to schedule the next get-together, take pictures, plan the menu, reserve the playing field, provide the entertainment? Choose a role you can play.

That's what Maria did when her family was planning a reunion. She knew there would be lots of food and lots of activity in the kitchen. Cooking had never been her strong point. She decided, "I need to find another role for myself or I am going to feel clumsy and out of place." She thought, "People love to eat, but they also love to be entertained." Maria decided to organize a game which involved guessing

the identities of family members from a description of
something they had done in their life. From young to old,
everyone enjoyed playing it. And Maria didn't worry about
having nothing to say. Her chosen role gave her plenty of
opportunities to speak up.

Choosing A Role Relieves Anxiety
One of the added benefits of consciously choosing a role for
yourself is that it will help relieve your feelings of anxiety and
inadequacy. Without a chosen role, no matter what you do in
a group, it is often not enough. Inside, you will still feel the
need to be more, say more, or shine more.

I remember experiencing just such fears when I contemplated
attending my college reunion. I thought, "I can't be with my
former classmates unless I'm perfect in every role imaginable
- perfect career, perfect shape, perfect relationship, etc.

I missed that reunion because I had not picked a realistic role
for myself. I was only thinking about how others would
evaluate me. What kind of conversation would that lead to?
"How do you like me so far?" Not a winning topic! I could
have said, "Let me try being an *Information Seeker*. There
will be so much to catch up on. Or, let me try being an
Includer. Many people will be there that I didn't know that
well in school and I'd like to talk with them." Choosing one
of those roles for myself might have gotten me to that reunion.

A Role Is Not You
Another advantage of role playing is that you know it is just a
role. It's not you - it is simply a part you are acting out with
this particular group. That gives you a tremendous amount of

freedom. Have fun with your roles. Experiment, and see what works and what doesn't.

Ryan was visiting a friend's family who were great story tellers. Each night after dinner, they would sit around the table and share tales from their childhood. There would be much laughing and joking. This was very different from Ryan's family. Their after dinner conversations were usually about serious political or philosophical subjects. Ryan thought, "Why not change from philosopher to story teller in this group? I won't be as good at it as they are since they've been doing this all their lives, but it will be fun to try. Besides, it's just a role I'm playing. It's not me who is being judged." Ryan became a story teller that night and even got a few laughs from the group. He enjoyed it. When you separate yourself from the roles you play in groups, you will be much less afraid of possible failure or rejection.

Sharon was running for an officer's position in an organization in which she was very active. Normally these positions were uncontested and the person who volunteered got the job. The year before, Sharon had run for the only position that had an opponent, and she lost. This year, once again, she was running for the only position that had an opponent. Would she lose again? How could she risk being rejected one more time from an organization that was made up of so many of her friends?

Sharon did not look at it that way. She said, "I'm running for office because I believe in what I can do. I figure at some point they'll have to elect me. If not, that's okay too." Sharon didn't look at her defeat as a rejection of herself. It was just a role for which she was running. Sharon won the second time around.

Try Different Roles

No matter what role you play in a group, remember to choose it yourself. You do not need to wait for the group to assign one to you. Take the initiative, find a role you want to try, and go for it. If it works well, congratulations, you have found a role that fits you. If it doesn't work out so well, you can try another role that will fit better.

Remember what Shakespeare said: "One man in his time will play many parts." Don't get stuck with the same part every time. Try out several roles. Learn from them. Taking on a role will give you an important, visible presence in a group. It will also make communicating in groups easier and more fun for you.

Summary Chapter 8

Smart Talk Key #8
Choose Your Role in the Group

- *Realize that everyone plays a role in groups*
- *Recognize that the leader is not the only role*
- *Take on a role to relieve anxiety*
- *Separate yourself from your role*
- *Try different roles*

Notes to Yourself:

Describe the role you have usually played in the past in group situations.

Choose a different role to play at your next group meeting, and write down the results.

Describe another role you would like to play in group situations.

Chapter 9
The Three P's -
Position, Power, Prestige

"Politics are almost as exciting as war, and
quite as dangerous. In war you can only be
killed once, but in politics many times."

Winston Churchill

Some people think politics is a dirty word and the less they
have to do with it, the better. One of the biggest complaints
employees have about their work environment is the office
politics with which they must contend. Many would rather
just do their job and not be bothered with the rest of it. But
politics cannot be avoided, especially when communicating.
No matter how adept you become at using the *smart talk* keys
we have been discussing in these chapters, if you apply them
without understanding the politics of your environment, you
are heading for disaster.

Stephanie, a manager of a book store, was interviewing candidates for a position she had open in her store. She was talking to a candidate's former employer. "He was a good worker and did his job well," this employer said, "but he wasn't very astute politically. He would say things that some people used against him later. He wasn't a trouble maker, just naive about how the business world works." That political naiveté was enough to jeopardize this person's job.

Politics is defined as the art of guiding or influencing decisions. We see it taking place openly at meetings when people try to win and hold control of the group. On the other hand, we often think of office politics as behind the scenes maneuvering, consisting of private rather than public conversations. We are not always sure who those people are, nor are we sure of what they are saying.

Being aware of politics does not mean you have to play politics. It is just like any other game - some people enjoy it and are good at it. Others are bored by it or have no talent for it. But whether you choose to play or not, you must understand enough about politics to keep out of trouble when communicating.

Position, Power, Prestige

The level of political influence a person has in a group generally depends on three things - their position, power, and prestige. The more someone has of these three P's, the more politically influential he or she is in the organization, whether it is a family, a corporation, an educational institution, or a group of friends.

What you need to understand is that the politically powerful person is usually going to exert more control over the communication process than the less powerful person. Just think back to when you were a child. In your conversations with your dad, your teacher, or your older brother or sister, who usually controlled the communication? Probably your dad, the teacher, or the older sibling. That is because they had more of the three P's than you had as a kid. When we reach adulthood, our communication is still affected by those three P's. The person in the group who has the higher position, power and prestige is still going to be in control of the communication process.

Peter had just joined a high tech firm as CFO and was puzzled by the management meetings he had to attend. He thought they were a waste of time. There was no set agenda, people talked and laughed throughout the whole meeting, and nothing seemed to be accomplished.

Rather than immediately voicing his opinion, he decided to try to figure out why these meetings were run as they were. He started with the boss and he soon had the answer. The boss was the founder of the company and had worked night and day for many years to get his business up and running. He still put in very long hours.

He used these staff meetings as a break from the constant pressure. For him they were a time when he could relax with employees he trusted. He enjoyed laughing and telling stories with his staff. He also thought it built company morale. Far from being unproductive, the boss saw these meetings as a sacred time to recharge and reconnect. Once Peter had figured out this political climate, he needed to adapt his no nonsense communication style to something more relaxed during those meetings.

Whenever you are confused about how a group is communicating, take a second look. Politics is probably influencing the flow of this communication. Before you speak up, you want to know who has the political power and who you might be offending.

You also want to know how much political power you desire in this particular group. Do not assume you want as much power as you can get. Richard Brislin, author of *The Art of Getting Things Done,* says people are generally motivated by one of three things:

- Power
- Affiliation
- Achievement

A person who is primarily motivated by power enjoys control and influence over people. A person who is primarily motivated by affiliation enjoys warm interactions with others. A person who is primarily motivated by achievement enjoys accomplishing challenging goals. Of course we each feel all three of these motivators in varying degrees, but it is helpful to identify our primary motivator. There is no right or wrong answer here. It is more a matter of personality and interest than anything else.

But knowing the answer can help you choose an appropriate communication style. If you seek affiliation, you need to emphasize *smart talk* key #2 in this book - Find common ground to build rapport. You will be looking for ways to connect and create opportunities for future relationships. If you seek achievement, you need to emphasize *smart talk* key #3 - Focus on the problem, not the person. You will be looking for the simplest, most direct way to solve the problem and then move on. If you seek power, you need to emphasize *smart talk* key # 8 - Choose you role in the group. You will be going after the leadership role, and will be looking for ways to control the direction of the group.

Avoid Non-Powerful Language

Although it may not be our primary motivator, we all want more power in a group at times, especially in the business arena. We would like our ideas to be taken seriously, and sometimes we want to influence or control a group's decision. Phyllis Mindell, Ph.D., in her book, *A Woman's Guide to the Language of Success,* gives some excellent advice on tipping the balance of power toward yourself when you are speaking. These guides can work for either men or women. When you want power she warns:

- *Never start a sentence with the word "I."* Instead of saying, "I think what we are trying to accomplish is..." say, "What we are trying to accomplish is..." Not leading with "I" gives you more authority. You are speaking for the group, not just for yourself.

- *Never use the word "Feel."* Instead of saying, "I feel this decision will have major ramifications," say, "This decision will have major ramifications." "Feel" is an emotion. It is subjective, changeable, unreliable. Leaving out that verb makes your message stronger, more definite and certain.

- *Never hedge.* Instead of saying "In my opinion, we need additional advertising dollars," say, "We need additional advertising dollars." Hedges reduce the credibility and power of your message. They weaken the point you are making.

Avoiding non-powerful phrases can help you gain more influence in a group. Taking advantage of powerful language when you speak will make a difference.

Create Your Own Image

Another technique for achieving more influence in a group is to create an image of yourself as a powerful person. Remember when you were young, your teachers and peers liked to fit you and your classmates into categories - "she's the brainy one, he's the athletic one, she's the popular one, etc." The same thing happens to us as adults. People create an image of us, and it often sticks to us, whether it is accurate or not. Kim Krisco, in his book *Leadership & the Art of Conversation,* suggests that we take control of our image by creating it ourselves rather than letting others create it for us.

Sally, a director of training and development, was serving on a committee in which she wanted more influence. However, as a relatively new member of the group, she didn't know how far she could push her ideas. Before she spoke up, she decided to create an image of herself as an innovator. Whenever she was talking with fellow staff members or her boss, she made sure to refer to herself with statements such as, "I like to stir things up to get new ideas out on the table," or, "I like bringing up controversial issues to get people to think out of the box." She was creating her own image as an innovative, forward thinking person, one who could lead a group in new directions.

By the time she began speaking up at the committee meetings, the other members had begun hearing and believing this image of her, and so rather than being offended at some new person spouting off opinions, they accepted her ideas more readily. They were expecting Sally to be innovative, and she was, because that was already the image they had of her in their minds.

Of course the image you create for yourself must match the reality of who you are and the talents you have. But rather than letting others create that image for you, try creating it for yourself. Use statements such as, "I like to get things done," or "I'm a good organizer," or "Creating something new is what really gets me excited." If you talk about the image you want to project, people will begin to accept that image, and they will give you more opportunity to use those talents to influence the group's direction.

The communication process will always be affected by those who have more position, power and prestige within the organization. To ignore that reality is foolish. How you relate to group politics is the key. In any communication situation, identify your primary motive. Are you looking for power, affiliation, or achievement? Then adjust your communication style to fit your motive. When you do that, you are using your awareness of politics to help you, rather than letting your lack of awareness hurt you.

Summary Chapter 9

Smart Talk Key #9
Understand Group Politics

- *Be aware of the power, position, and prestige of the people in your group*
- *Recognize that a powerful person exerts more control over communication*
- *Identify what motivates you - power, affiliation, or achievement*
- *Avoid non-powerful language*
- *Create your own image*

Notes to Yourself:

Describe the politics of one group you are in. Who have the power, prestige, position?

Identify your chief motivator in this group. Do you want power, affiliation, or achievement?

Create an image of yourself that matches the talents you have. What phrases would you use with other people to promote that image?

Part 3

Smart Talk
at Large Gatherings

Chapter 10
Knowing Why Helps

"The purpose of life is a life of purpose."
Robert Byrne

The event is marked on your calendar. You have RSVP'd
that you will be attending. Many people in your industry will
be there. Why are you now, two days before the event, trying
to think of any excuse not to attend? And you do have some
good ones (excuses, that is). "The evening will be boring. I
don't know anyone else going. The alcohol and hor d'oerves
aren't good for my diet. I hate small talk. I could get a lot
more done working at the office, etc., etc."

Don't be surprised at these feelings of ambivalence. You are
experiencing a common ailment. It's called minglephobia - a
dread of mingling with a large group of people, many of
whom you don't even know. Your hesitation is perfectly
understandable. And yet we are asked to mingle every time

we attend trade meetings, conventions, conferences, charity events, social hours, weddings, or reunions. Knowing how to communicate at large gatherings such as these is an important skill for you to master.

The first question you need to ask yourself is, "Why am I going to this event?" If the answer is, "Because I have to," you'll need to come up with another reason. It may be true that you have to go. Perhaps it's a company meeting you must attend, or a friend's wedding you cannot miss. In those cases, you don't have a choice. You must show up. However, "because I have to go" is not a strong enough reason to make you successful. In fact, if that is your only reason, it will predict your failure.

Carolyn was attending the opening night social hour at her profession's annual convention. She didn't particularly want to be there, but her company required everyone to attend. She dreaded having to go through the motions of pretending to be interested in conversations she'd heard a hundred times before. As soon as she entered the ball room, she searched for her co-workers who were also attending. She spent the whole evening with that group. At the end of the night, she went up to her hotel room thinking, "What a waste of time. And I have to go through three more days of this."

Contrast Carolyn's experience with Annette's, who attended the same convention. Annette was new to the industry and excited to meet people in her profession. At the opening night social hour, she spent a few minutes with co-workers from her company, and then set off to introduce herself to other attendees. She met people from New York City, Minneapolis, San Diego, and Seattle. She talked to CEO's, financial managers, and strategic planners. She exchanged business cards with several people with whom she wanted to keep in touch after the meetings. Going up to her hotel room that evening, she said to herself, "What a great night. I can hardly wait for the next three days."

The difference in Carolyn's and Annette's experience that evening was not due to their mingling skills. They were both personable, intelligent, and articulate. It was rather due to the difference in their motivation levels for being there. Carolyn had no motivation except that she "had to be there." Annette, on the other hand, had considerable motivation. She wanted to meet people within her profession, she wanted to share ideas with them, and she wanted to make contacts for the future.

Choose a "Why" for Being There

Whenever you are getting ready to attend a large gathering, whether it's business or social, the key is the same. *Identify a purpose for attending.* It must be a purpose that motivates you, and one upon which you can act. Everyone has to find their own particular "why" for mingling. Here are three which may start you thinking:

1. Mingle for Information
Pick several topics that you are interested in at the moment. They can be business, recreational, philosophical, etc. Here is a list you might come up with:
- Running a marathon
- Traveling in Africa
- Career transitions

Now you could go to the library, the bookstore, or the internet to get information on these topics. But what better resource could you have than talking with a lot of different people and getting their perspective.

Scott, a sales engineer for an office equipment distributor, was attending an industry trade show. He had been attending this show for years, and although the new technology was always interesting to see, he wasn't looking forward to the trip. "I feel so uncomfortable with all those people," he thought to himself. "I never know what to say to most of them."

Scott was packing his running shoes, because he had a goal of running a marathon. He didn't know anything about training for one since he had never run anything longer than a 10k. Scott decided to use this trade show as a chance to learn all he could about marathon training. He began to bring the subject up when he was talking to colleagues and potential customers.

He was amazed at the response. Almost everyone knew someone who had trained for a marathon, or had run one themselves. He began to collect some good information. He discovered web sites, books, and magazines to read. He got advice about what to eat, how much to run, and what marathon to try first.

Scott actually began to look forward to his conversations with people. He was mingling with a purpose, and because of that, he was enjoying himself and making good contacts at the same time.

2. Mingle for Practice
A large gathering is a great place to practice your communication skills. You have the chance to use many of the skills we have been discussing in this book, including:

- Listening
- Nodding or chuckling
- Bridging
- Story telling

The great thing about large gatherings is that you have a chance to talk with so many different groups of people in just one evening. If you make a mistake once, you can try it again on the next group and see if you do better.

Joyce was making a move within her company from customer service to sales. In her new job, she would be calling on many people and would need to establish rapport with them quickly. Joyce wanted to get some communication practice before she did it for real in front of customers. She started looking for opportunities to meet new people. She began attending her local chamber of commerce meetings and after work social hours. The chamber was an organization her company had always belonged to, but Joyce had never taken the time to attend. Now she had a motivation. At these meetings she practiced introducing herself, listening, making eye contact, nodding, smiling, and maybe even telling a story from her life. By using these non-critical environments for rehearsal, Joyce became more confident in her communication skills, and was soon ready to call on customers.

3. Mingle for Fun

A third reason for attending large gatherings is just for fun. Mingling is the lightest kind of discourse there is. You are not trying to solve problems, put out fires, or sell your ideas. You are just playing a conversational game. Each player adds his or her own particular flair, and there are no winners or losers. Everyone can just get out there and take a conversational swing. If you miss, there's no harm in trying again.

Prepare an Agenda

Mingling for information, for practice, and for fun are just three reasons that might motivate you. You can come up with many other ideas of your own.   In their book *Great Connections,* authors Anne Baber and Lynne Waymon suggest writing out an actual agenda for your purpose. What do you want to get and what do you want to give? Getting is what you want to learn from other people. Giving is what other people can learn from you.

What you want to get might be:
- how to market yourself
- how to build a deck
- how to job hunt on the internet.

What you want to give could be:
- how to travel inexpensively in Europe
- how to create a financial plan
- how to design a web site

When you have something to get and something to give, it can make for a lively and satisfying interchange for everyone involved.

Remember, identifying a purpose for attending a large gathering is crucial to your success there. If you have a powerful, motivating "why" for doing something, the "how" will often take care of itself. This is true for anything you want in life. It is especially true for enjoying your mingling opportunities.

Summary for Chapter 10

Smart Talk Key #10
Always Have a Purpose For Attending

- *Choose a "why" for attending any gathering*
- *Mingle for information, practice, fun*
- *Prepare an agenda for what you want to get and give*

Notes To Yourself:

Choose a purpose for attending an upcoming large gathering you have on your calendar

List   three topics of interest for which you might seek information at a mingling event.

Prepare an agenda for what you want to get and give at your next mingling opportunity.

Chapter 11
Overcoming Your Fears

"If all that Americans want is security, then they can go to prison. They'll have enough to eat, a bed, and a roof over their heads."

Dwight D. Eisenhower

Once you've identified your purpose for attending a large gathering, you may still feel hesitant about going. You might be thinking - "I can't walk into a roomful of people I don't know, and just start talking with them. How would I approach them? What would I say? And what if they don't want to talk to me? What if they ignore me? I could be left standing alone with everyone staring at me. That would be just too embarrassing."

Don't worry, these are all common fears of mingling, and they can be overcome. Let's look at these fears one at a time

I Can't Talk to a Roomful of People I Don't Know

At most events, even if you don't know the people, you will all be there for some common purpose. Perhaps you are a member of the same profession or organization, a friend of the bride or groom, or enrolled in the same class, etc. That makes these people less than total strangers. You have a connection with them which you can use when you approach someone to initiate a conversation.

Janet goes to an aerobics class almost every night after work. These classes are full of people she doesn't know. But are they strangers that she can't approach? No, they all have a common purpose for being there. They are all interested in working out and keeping in shape. It would be perfectly appropriate for her to say to the person next to her, "Do you know the name of this instructor? I like her routine."

At business functions, you are expected to talk to people you don't know. Companies and organizations spend a lot of time, effort, and money sponsoring conventions, conferences, trade shows, seminars, retreats, etc. at the local, national, and even international level. Why do you think they do that? So everyone will stick to themselves and talk only to people they already know? That's not likely their intent. They want people to mingle, meet new clients, get fresh ideas, stay on top of what's happening in the industry. That can only happen if people talk to other people they haven't met yet.

Social functions also work better when those attending talk with other people they don't know. How many times have you been to a wedding where all the groom's family and friends sit on one side of the reception hall, and all the bride's family and friends sit on the other. One of the purposes of a wedding is to bring these two sets of family and friends together. It would not only be appropriate but appreciated by the bride and groom if the two groups talked with each other.

So don't be afraid to talk to people you don't know. When you are attending a business or social gathering in which all of you are there for a shared purpose, you are missing out on the whole intent of the event if you don't.

How Can I Approach Strangers?

Many people would at least like an introduction before they attempt to talk to people they don't know. It would be nice if at large gatherings there would be a host or hostess ready to take you around the room and introduce you to everyone, but that rarely happens. You're usually on your own. Rather than waiting to be introduced, author Susan RoAne, in her book *How To Work a Room*, suggests practicing and delivering a self-introduction. Prepare one that is short and to the point. Give your name and something about yourself that helps define your connection to the group.

If you are at an industry meeting, your professional position and the company you're with would be appropriate. "Hello, I'm Matt Erickson, financial analyst for Anderson & Associates." If you are at a book signing party, how you know the author would be more fitting. "Hello, I'm Matt Erickson. Sarah, the author, is my cousin."

Notice Matt changes his self-introduction to fit the occasion. In each case, he explains his connection to the event. After Matt gives the other person an opportunity to introduce themselves, it would be helpful if he gave a piece of additional information that could be used as a springboard to carry the conversation along. At the industry meeting, he might say, "My boss, Jim Anderson, usually represents our firm at these meetings. This is the first time I've attended." At the book signing he might say, "I used to love visiting Sarah when we were kids. Her family raised Morgan horses, and she gave me riding lessons." These added pieces of information give the other person something to respond to, and make it easier to continue the conversation.

Another way to help you overcome your fear of approaching people is to adopt what Susan RoAne calls *host rather than guest behavior*. Think of the role of a host or hostess. A good one practices gracious manners, starts conversations, introduces people, and tries to make all guests feel comfortable. In short, they extend themselves more than the guests to make sure the party is successful. If you adopt that mindset, you will graciously take the initiative rather than wait for someone to approach you.

Dave was attending his industry's trade show. He was standing at a buffet line in the large ball room, and decided to use host behavior to initiate a conversation with the person behind him. "Do you like shrimp? It looks like they are almost out. I don't eat them myself. If you'd like to go ahead of me, you're welcome to." Dave was showing gracious manners and concern for a fellow guest.

Other host comments might be:
- "I'm going to get a drink. May I get something for you?"
- "I'm heading over to the buffet line. Would you like to join me?"
- "I'd like to introduce you to our CEO - she would be interested in talking with you."

A good host or hostess does everything they can to make their guests feel comfortable. If you adopt that mindset, you will have less fear of approaching people. In fact, you will want to help them have an enjoyable evening.

What If People Don't Want to Talk to Me?

Finally we come to the biggest fear of all when mingling. What if your initiative is rejected? What if the person or the group makes it clear they don't want to talk to you? Just thinking about that possibility feels painful. None of us like to put ourselves in the position of potential rejection. And when we're attempting to mingle with many new people, that is certainly a possibility.

There may be times when we will get a cold shoulder or cold look from a group or individual we approach. If that happens, it's smart to move on with your composure intact. A simple, "Excuse me, won't you?," or, "Excuse me, I don't want to interrupt," is the best response. Don't try to escalate the situation by forcing yourself onto the group. Just walk away.

But walk away where? It's best to have a destination in mind. And it shouldn't be your hotel room or home, even though that's where you may feel like going. Give yourself a chance to compose yourself. Take a breath, put on a smile, and perhaps head for the food or drink line. You don't have to actually get anything. It's just a comfortable place to survey the room, and start up a conversation with someone there.

That well-known advice, "Don't take it personally," is especially applicable in these situations. After all, these people don't know you. So they couldn't be rejecting you personally. It is much more likely that they were in a group that just didn't want to admit any strangers. It would have disrupted their comfort level. It has nothing to do with you.

We have looked at three of the most common fears that keep people from mingling. There is no need for us to be stopped by these fears. We can talk to a roomful of people with whom we share a common purpose, we can introduce ourselves rather than waiting to be introduced, we can adopt host rather than guest behavior, and we can respond to rejection without taking it personally. Booker T. Washington said, "You measure the size of the accomplishment by the obstacles you had to overcome to reach your goals." Every time you overcome these fears of mingling and go out and do it anyway, you can be proud of your accomplishment. You are proving to yourself that you can be a successful communicator in any situation.

Summary for Chapter 11

Smart Talk Key #11
Overcome Your Fears of Mingling

- *Identify the common group purpose*
- *Introduce yourself*
- *Take the initiative*
- *Don't take rejection personally*

Notes to Yourself:

List three large events you have attended or will attend. Write
down the common purpose of each.

Prepare an introduction of yourself that would be appropriate
for a business function.

Describe what you would say and do if a person or group you
approached did not respond to your initiative.

Notes:

Chapter 12
How to Work
the Room

*"The first and great commandment is,
Don't let them scare you."*

Elmer Davis

You have now arrived at the gathering and are standing at the entrance into that room of talking, laughing people. What do you do next, besides turning around and going home?

Taking your initial steps into a roomful of people you don't know can be intimidating. Where should you go, who should you approach, what should you say? Unless you have a plan, you are going to feel at a loss. Take a quick survey of the room before walking in. Pretend to be looking for someone. Scan the room with your eyes and locate these three things:

- The hosts or sponsors of the party
- The food and beverage areas
- The people you recognize

1. Host or Sponsor of the Party

It is not only polite to greet the host or sponsor of the party when you arrive, it gives you a destination when you enter the room. Express your pleasure to be there, your appreciation for their giving the party, and your admiration for something about the gathering - the people, the food, the decor, etc. When the host of the party is a company or organization, the employees of that company are the hosts, so express your appreciation to them. Often they are required by their organization to be there and mingle, and they would like nothing better than to have a guest come up and express appreciation to them.

2. Food and Beverage Areas

Food and drink are served at parties for another reason besides feeding hungry or thirsty guests. They are a vehicle for socializing. When you meet with friends or family, think how often the occasion is for dinner, lunch, or a cup of coffee. Food and drink offer a reason for getting together. They oil the socializing machine. Take advantage of this at a large gathering and use the food and drink areas to help you start mingling.

When you first arrive at a party, heading for the drink or food area gives you a destination. Standing in line is an ideal place to introduce yourself to the person in front or behind you. Commenting on the food or drink is an easy way to start a conversation. Sipping on a glass of wine or a glass of water puts something in your hand, which helps relieve the awkwardness of simply having your hands hanging at your sides.

It's not advisable to have both hands full - one with a drink, one with food. That severely limits your ability to maneuver and greet people. I would suggest starting with a drink, mingling awhile, and then visiting the food table. That will give you another destination for later in the evening.

3. People You Recognize
If you see a few familiar faces in the crowd, that's a great place to start your mingling. Even if the face is just slightly familiar - perhaps you've seen them at other functions you've attended - you can use that as a reason for introducing yourself. Bring up the past occasion, and see if there is a connection. They will be complimented that you remembered their face. When you find business associates or friends at the party, you can start your mingling with them, but don't stick with friends the whole evening. Your purpose is to meet new people, so venture out or invite new people into your conversational group.

Even with a destination in mind, entering the room may still feel intimidating to you. Jeanne Martinet, who wrote *The Art of Mingling*, recommends using mental fantasies during those first few awkward moments when you enter a room. The self-confidence you project is more important than what you might be feeling inside at that moment. Here are three of Martinet's fantasies you might want to try:

1. The Invisible Man
The invisible man is easy. You pretend just what it says - to be invisible. When you walk around the room you can see other people, but they can't see you. That means you don't have to be self-conscious. You can glide through the room without anyone noticing you.

Michelle did just that when she had to attend a large industry-wide cocktail reception. She decided to walk across the room to the refreshment tables pretending to be invisible. She didn't try to make eye contact with anyone or join a particular group. She just walked and looked around, observing the color and style of dress, the size and gender mixture of groups, the level and tone of conversations. She amazed herself by making it across the room without feeling in the least self-conscious. In fact, it was almost fun. She felt free to be curious and observant, without worrying about peoples' reactions to her.

2. Buddy System

Anyone who has socialized with a date and without a date has experienced the value of the buddy system. I remember going to large gatherings alone without a date. My stomach would have butterflies in it and I would have to push myself to walk into the room. With a date, that nervousness didn't come up. It seemed easy. We just walked in together.

What Martinet suggests is creating an imaginary buddy for yourself. Don't use a real buddy, because mingling is better done solo. But pretending to have that favorite friend on your side when you enter the room, encouraging you, supporting you, and telling you that you're the best thing that happened to this party, is perfectly okay.

3. Celebrity Persona

Another fantasy is to take on the persona of a celebrity you admire. Walk into the room as if you were quarterback star John Elway or Olympic swimmer Amy Van Dyken. You are not self-conscious, because as a celebrity, you are used to big crowds admiring you, asking for your autograph. You are naturally gracious and kind to everyone.

Moving From One Group to Another

Once you have gotten yourself into the room, spoken with the host or sponsor, chatted while in line for a drink, and perhaps initiated a conversation with a familiar face, you are well on your way to a successful night of mingling. At that point, you can use the techniques we have discussed in previous chapters for talking one-on-one and in small groups - find common ground to build rapport (Chapter 2), listen with a purpose (Chapter 4), show support for others' topics (Chapter 5), give everyone a turn to speak (Chapter 6) and introduce your own topics (Chapter 7).

The big difference in communicating at a large gathering is that you will not be staying with one person or group for the whole evening. Instead you will be moving from group to group, talking with many different people. That is the purpose of large gatherings. You are missing the point of the party or the convention if you stick with one group all night. Spending fifteen to thirty minutes in one place (depending on the size of the party), and then moving on, is appropriate. Many of us look for a group we can easily join, and then attach ourselves there for the rest of the night. That is not mingling.

So how do you exit from one group and gracefully move on to the next? Simply have a clear idea of where you are going next and express that. Food, drink, restroom, and telephone are common departure destinations.

"Excuse me, I'm going to check out the buffet line"
"Excuse me, I'm going to freshen up my drink."
"Excuse me, I'm going to use the restroom."
"Excuse me, I need to make a telephone call."

End all of these exits with something like -
"It was so nice talking with you," or, "I enjoyed meeting you."
And off you go. Before you know it, you'll be moving around the room like a pro.

What To Talk About All Evening

Even though you know how to enter a roomful of people, and how to move from group to group, you might still be asking yourself, "What am I going to talk about all evening?" This is where preparation for the event comes in. If you know you are going to be meeting a wide variety of people, it would make sense to come prepared with a variety of subjects to talk about.

Some of you have heard the phrase: "Great minds discuss ideas, average minds discuss events, small minds discuss people." I suggest most of us are interested in all three of these subjects - ideas, events and people. Each of them can make great topics of conversation. You just need to prepare.

You gather information about ideas, events and people from what you read, what you hear, what you see, and what you experience. Some of you will be more comfortable with one medium than with another. That's okay. One is not better than the other. Just make sure you are continually refreshing your mind with new information.

What You Read

A good place to start reading is your city's daily newspaper. You have seasoned professionals putting together local, regional and national news for you every day. The business, sports, entertainment, and editorial sections are full of stories about ideas, events and people that you can talk about. USA Today, The Wall Street Journal, and the New York Times are good choices for national and international news.

Besides your local paper, it would be advantageous for you to read a general magazine such as Time or a business magazine such as Forbes or Fortune. Here again, you have professional editors putting together for you the top stories of the moment about people, events, and ideas. This is a rich source for your conversations. Reading your industry periodicals and newsletters is also important to keep up with what is going on in your field.

What You Hear and See

For those of you who are more auditory, the radio can be a source of ideas. News, talk, and sports stations will be most helpful in giving you opinions and interviews to talk about. Books on tape are another auditory way to enlarge your range of topics. If you are primarily visual, TV and cable programming offer many sources of information. And, of course, the internet is now a vast, world-wide source on any subject.

The problem for us today is not lack of information, it is lack of time to absorb the information. Rather than try to cover everything, I recommend you choose one or two of your favorite mediums and make it a habit to use them every day.

What You Experience

The people, events, and ideas you experience first-hand are often your richest source of material for conversation. Whenever I am in the midst of learning a new sport, taking a class, joining an organization, or working on a new project, I am suddenly a much more dynamic conversationalist. I can feel it in the way I relate to people and how they relate to me. Why is that? It is simply because I am excited about the things I'm doing in my life. Therefore I enjoy talking about them. And I look forward to hearing what other people are doing and how their insights might apply to me. So in your search for information on people, events and ideas, don't forget that you are your own best source. Keep that source nourished and growing by pursuing new things that keep you excited about life.

In this chapter we've talked about how to enter a room, how to move from group to group, and how to find something to talk about. Mingling at a large gathering is meant to be an opportunity to enjoy, not a crisis to avoid. It is a lighthearted, conversational game. There are no winners or losers. The only losers are those who never try it. So walk into that room and mingle. You can do it.

Summary for Chapter 12

Smart Talk Key #12
Enter With Courage, Exit With Grace

- *Have a destination when you enter the room*
- *Don't get stuck in one place*
- *Prepare topics to discuss beforehand*

Notes To Yourself:

Describe how you would work the room at your next large gathering.

What media sources are you going to use for information about people, events, and ideas. When will you use them?

List two new experiences in your life that are keeping you fresh.

Notes:

Chapter 13
The Final Key
To Success

*"If you asked me what I came into this world to do,
I will tell you: I came to live out loud."*

Emile Zola

Congratulations. You now possess the twelve *smart talk* keys for helping you say the right thing at the right time. You have the skills to be recognized and rewarded when you are talking one-on-one, in small groups, and at large gatherings. Let's review those twelve keys:

Part 1: Smart Talk One-On-One

1. Appreciate What Is Unique About You
- Search for your own communication style
- Focus on your unique qualities
- Draw from your life experiences
- Don't try to imitate others

2. *Find Common Ground To Build Rapport*
- Use the situation, other person, or yourself for conversation starters
- Use bridges and transitions to keep the conversation going
- Don't use questions to change the subject

3. *Focus On the Problem, Not the Person*
- Find a point of agreement
- Distance yourself from the personal
- Talk in terms of the problem

4. *Listen*
- Recognize that listening is as important as speaking
- Have a purpose for listening
- Slow down
- Don't be afraid of silence

Part 2: Smart Talk In Groups

5. *Show Support For Others' Topics*
- Look at the speaker
- Nod your head
- Laugh or chuckle
- Ask a speaker to continue
- Avoid a deadpan facial expression
- Don't contradict the speaker

6. Give Everyone a Turn To Speak
- Let the current speaker choose the next speaker
- Give each person an equal number of turns
- Hand people their turn when appropriate
- Don't interrupt
- Don't keep a turn too long

7. Step Into the Spotlight
- Speak up early
- Prepare your point and example
- Know how to tell stories
- Introduce topics you are excited about

8. Choose Your Role In the Group
- Realize that everyone plays a role in groups
- Recognize that the leader is not the only role
- Take on a role to relieve anxiety
- Separate yourself from your role
- Try different roles

9. Understand Group Politics
- Be aware of the position, power, and prestige of the people in your group
- Recognize that a powerful person exerts more control over any communication
- Identify what motivates you - power, affiliation, or achievement
- Avoid non-powerful language
- Create your own image

Part 3: Smart Talk At Large Gatherings

10. Always Have a Purpose For Attending
- Choose a *why* for attending any gathering
- Mingle for information, practice, fun
- Prepare an agenda for what you want to get and give

11. Overcome Your Fears of Mingling
- Identify the common group purpose
- Introduce yourself
- Take the initiative
- Don't take rejection personally

12. Enter With Courage, Exit With Grace
- Have a destination when you enter the room
- Don't get stuck in one place
- Prepare topics to discuss beforehand

I encourage you to practice these skills every day. That means taking a small risk every day. Initiate a conversation instead of letting the opportunity slip by. Speak up early at your next business meeting instead of remaining silent. Smile, nod, and laugh when listening rather than appearing expressionless. With each risk you take, you will be stepping toward your goal of becoming a successful communicator.

A step at a time requires just a small effort. But added together, those steps will create a big result. You will be "living your life out loud" by expressing yourself to the rest of the world and saying the right thing at the right time. I can't think of a greater accomplishment or a more important one. Becoming a *smart* communicator is a high challenge that offers great rewards. Only you can finally discover that for yourself.

"Surely a man has come to himself," said Woodrow Wilson, "only when he has found the best that is in him and has satisfied his heart with the highest achievement he is fit for."

Finding your best is a lifetime adventure. May you discover and develop the best communicator inside you, and use that power to help yourself and others *"live out loud."*

The Final Smart Talk Key
One Step at a Time

"Perseverance is not a long race; it is many short races one after another."

Walter Elliott

Notes:

Bibliography

Baber, Anne/Waymon, Lynne. *Great Connections.*
Manassas Park, VA: Impact Publications, 1992.

Brislin, Richard W. *The Art of Getting Things Done.* New
York: Praeger Publishers, 1991.

Elgin, Suzzette Haden, Ph.D. *Genderspeak.* New York:
J. Wiley, 1993.

Garner, Alan. *Conversationally Speaking.* New York:
McGraw-Hill, 1981.

Krisco, Kim. *Leadership & the Art of Conversation.*
Rocklin, CA: Prima Publishing, 1997.

Martinet, Jeanne. *The Art of Mingling.* New York:
St. Martin's Press, 1992.

Mindell, Phyllis, Ph.D. *A Woman's Guide to the Language
of Success.* Englewood Cliffs, NJ: Prentice Hall, 1995.

Rees, Fran. *Teamwork from Start to Finish.* San Francisco,
CA: Pfeiffer, 1997.

RoAne, Susan. *How to Work a Room.* New York: Warner
Books, 1989.

Tannen, Deborah, Ph.D. *Talking from 9 to 5.* New York:
Avon Books, 1994.

About the Author

Dawn Lehman, M.S., M.B.A., has eighteen years of experience as a manager and vice president in the media industry. Along the way she has learned about the nuances of business communication from the inside out. With Masters Degrees in Radio/TV and Business Administration, she is uniquely qualified to help individuals and organizations master their communication challenges. She lives in Denver, Colorado.

If you or your company are interested in additional copies of *Smart Talk,* or information on the speaking services which Dawn Lehman provides, please contact:

DawnLehman@aol.com

or

Dawn Lehman & Associates
1555 S. Syracuse St.
Denver, CO
303-750-1139

Notes:

Notes:

Notes:

Notes: